D1551514

Amazon Echo Dot 2nd Generation:
Learn To Work With Your Echo Dot And Make Your Life Easier

Table of content

Introduction:

Amazon Echo Dot has a length of about 9.25 inch tall and the shape of the speaker is just like a cylinder having a microphone array of 7 pieces. Amazon Echo Dot is a kind of small speaker which has many built in capabilities. Amazon Echo retorts to the similar phrase which is called wake phrase "Alexa" and has the ability of voice interplay, controlling compatible smart devices, music playback from several instruments through the Bluetooth, it also has the ability to make the to do lists, streaming podcasts, set the alarms, offering weather forecasts, enjoying audiobooks, reading PDFs, answering trivialities, warn you about the traffic stipulations, and supplying different forms of knowledge in real time. It might additionally have a linked with your speakers through the Bluetooth or along with the audio cable. The tap, Echo, and Dot are very equivalent speakers that have been discussed in this eBook.

Echo needs the web connection for working efficiently. The voice of Amazon Dot Echo awareness capacity is established on Amazon net offerings and the Amazon long established voice platform it received from Evi, Yap, and IVONA and the Polish situated specialist in voice expertise used in the Kindle fire. The present world of the interlinked homes remains to be very detached mess. As Google and Apple compete with their own requirements and other corporations are working the same with their own perspective Amazon has very snuck within the attractive, part door with its sensible speaker. Other than that it also acts as a substitute, speakers.

Chapter 01 -- Amazon Echo Dot – An Introduction

Amazon Echo which is also called as mission D or Doppler and shortened and known as Echo is a speaker and is designed through Amazon. Amazon Echo includes a 23.5 cm which is approx. 9.25 - inch speaker which has a shape like cylinder with a seven piece microphone display. The device retorts to the title "Alexa". This "wake phrase" will also be modified through the consumer to both "Amazon" and "Echo".

Amazon Echo is ready of music playback, voice interaction, and creation of to do lists, atmosphere alarms, enjoying audiobooks, streaming podcasts and offering climate, visitors and different actual time information. It may also control a few devices utilizing itself as an automation hub.

Amazon manufacturer had been establishing inside Echo of its Lab126 places of work in Cambridge and Massachusetts, Silicon Valley, due to the fact at the least 2010 in definite levels of reports. This gadget used to be the part of Amazon that makes an attempt to develop its gadget portfolio before the e-reader known as Kindle. The Echo was featured in the first-ever tremendous Bowl Amazon e-reader advert in 2016.

Echo was in the beginning restrained to Amazon prime individuals or via invitation, however grew to become extensively on hand in the US on 23th June, 2015. Speculated press that would create its Canadian in the year 2016 after Amazon posted job listings for builders for the co-hosted, Alexa and hackathon. The Echo grew to be accessible in the UK on September 28th, 2016. Additionally, the Alexa voice provider is accessible to be introduced to different instruments and different organizations' services and instruments are inspired to link to it.

Operation Overview:

In the default mode the Amazon Echo constantly adapt to all discourse, monitoring for the word wake, which is specifically mounted as "Alexa" derived from Alexa web, the Amazon possessed web indexing organization. This device additionally comes up with a voice activated and physically far off manipulates which might be used in lieu of the ' word wake '. Microphones of Echo's will also be automatically disabled through urgent a mute button to display the audio processing unit.

Echo needs the web connection as a way to work. The voice of Amazon Echo awareness capacity is established on Amazon net offerings and the Amazon long established voice platform it received from Yap, Evi, and IVONA and the Polish situated specialist in voice expertise used in the Kindle fire.

Echo achieves good with a 'just right' that is low latency web connection which reduces processing time due to nominal verbal exchange round journeys, stream able retorts and geo dispensed carrier endpoints.

Echo agreements climate from the app of AccuWeather and information from a type of bases, together with neighborhood NPR, radio stations and ESPN from TuneIn. Amazon Echo can play track from owner of Amazon track debts and has built-in support for the Spotify and Pandora streaming tune offerings and has maintenance for Nest Thermostats and IFTTT. Echo may additionally play tune from streaming services comparable to Apple music, and Google Play track from a mobilephone or tablet. Echo maintains voice-controlled timers, alarms, browsing and to do lists and might admittance Wikipedia articles. Amazon Echo will reply to the users' questions about gadgets for the calendar of Google. It additionally integrates with Philips Hue, Yonomi, SmartThings, Belkin Wemo and Insteon, and Wink. As well as the integration with the Amazon Echo is in the works for Countertop by way of Scout Alarm, Orange Chef, Garageio, MARA, Toymail, and Mojio.

It might not be easy to show up to be the competent of track streamed from a local DLNA/ UPnP mass media server.

Add Alexa to any room

Amazon Echo also has entry to knowledge constructed with the help of Alexa talents kit. These are 3rd occasion advanced voice involvements that add to the competences of any

Alexa enabled device for instance the Echo. Examples of capabilities comprise the potential to play sound, set an alarm, answer normal questions, order a pizza, Uber, and more. Capabilities are constantly being brought to expand the capabilities accessible to the consumer. The Alexa expertise package is a group of self-carrier APIs, documentation, tools, and code samples that adapt it as fast and easy as for any developer to add competencies to Alexa. Developers may additionally use the "smart dwelling ability API", a new count to the Alexa potential package, to deprived of trouble instruct Alexa tips on how to control cloud skillful lighting and thermostat contraptions. All of the programs execute in the cloud - nothing is on any consumer gadget. A designer can follow tutorials to gain knowledge of speedily build voice involvements for his or her new and current submissions.

Echo Dot device is a type of voice-controlled, hands-free device that act similar as the far-field voice consciousness as Amazon Echo. Amazon Dot is a kind of small speaker which is built in — it might additionally have a linked with your speakers through the Bluetooth or along with the audio cable. Amazon Dot have a strong connection with the Alexa Voice provider to play certain types of music, gives information, information, sporting events ratings, information of climate, and extra— as immediately as possible.

Echo Dot is able to hear you from the room, even when some song is playing in the room. When you wish to have to use the Amazon Echo Dot, simply say the wake phrase "Alexa" and the Amazon Dot will reply immediately. When you have an Echo more than one or Echo Dot, Alexa retorts perceptively from the Amazon Echo gadget you're much closest to the term of ESP (Echo Spatial belief).

Chapter 02 -- Features of Amazon Echo Dot

Amazon Echo has a length of about 9.25 – inch tall and the shape of the speaker is just like a cylinder having a 7 piece microphone array. Amazon Echo retorts to the similar phrase which is called wake phrase "Alexa" and has the ability of voice interplay, controlling compatible smarthome devices, music playback from several instruments through the Bluetooth, also have the ability to make the to do lists, streaming podcasts, set the alarms, enjoying audiobooks, offering weather forecasts, reading PDFs, answering trivialities, warn you about the traffic stipulations, and supplying different forms of knowledge in actual time.

Echo needs a Wi-Fi connection just to reply to voice instructions and while getting content for the user, and it have to stay plugged in for vigor. Customers in the USA will view the wake phrase Alexa that the accent of America, whilst all the UK customers would be able to hear a British accent.

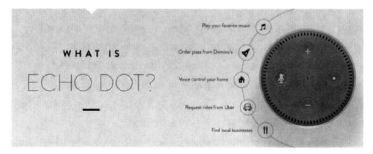

Features of Amazon Echo Dot:

1. Echo Dot of the Amazon lineup several offers which is usually tiered-speaker and the heights that remind the customers of Starbucks espresso sizes (venti, grande, along with the trenta).

2. Enterprise creates a cylindrical shaped, web-connected speaker referred to as Echo, which doubles as a cloud assistant, personal, titled as Alexa. It launched in the America in the year of 2015 and it launched into Europe and the United Kingdom in the very next year i.e. 2016.

3. In conjunction with the Amazon Echo Dot, Amazon also presents two audio systems which are debuted in the year of March 2016 in the United States, referred to as Echo Dot or Amazon tap, the latter terms of these devices has now been changed with a new and highly updated mannequin. The Amazon tap presently not available in the UK.

4. Make all three speakers and place them next to each other, beginning with the Echo and ending with the Dot, and the user will get one very tall, one little medium, and one very short.

5. The variations among the audio system of Amazon are not constrained to top though; each one is highly sophisticated and much suitable to a certain atmosphere – whether it would be placed at home, or as an enhancement to your present setup of the audio system or on the go.

6. Amazon Dot is a kind of small speaker which is built in — it might additionally have a linked with your speakers through the Bluetooth or along with the audio cable. Amazon Dot have a strong connection with the Alexa Voice provider to play certain types of music, gives information, information, sporting events ratings, information of climate, and extra— as immediately as possible.

7. Echo Dot is able to hear you from the room, even when some song is playing in the room. When you wish to have to use the Amazon Echo Dot, simply say the wake phrase "Alexa" and the Amazon Dot will reply immediately.

8. When you have an Echo more than one or Echo Dot, Alexa retorts perceptively from the Amazon Echo gadget you're much closest to the term of ESP.

9. In a slightly display or any type of creepy interface of semi-AI, the Echo is continually linked to Alexa of Amazon network, which is included in the cloud and consistently getting more and more smarter.

10. The extra you utilize it, the extra it learns your speech patterns, preferences, and vocabulary, to raised give on what the user would requesting. It would be constantly learning.

11. Amazon Echo is ready of music playback, voice interaction, and creation of to do lists, atmosphere alarms, enjoying audiobooks, streaming podcasts and offering climate, visitors and different actual time information.
12. It may also control a few devices utilizing itself as an automation hub.

Other important features of Amazon Echo are as follows:

1. **Availability of the Amazon Echo** = Available in United States (Amazon United States order page) and also Available in the country of United Kingdom (Amazon United Kingdom order page)
2. **Release date in United States and United** Kingdom = in United States = 2015, in United Kingdom = 2016 .
3. **Dimensions** = 235 millimeter x 83.5 millimeter x 83.5 millimeter
4. Price of Amazon Echo = in United States = $179, in United Kingdom = £149
5. **Weight of Amazon Echo** = 1045 in grams
6. **Power** = Plugs in any outlet of wall
7. **Connectivity of Amazon Echo with other devices** = Dual-band, Bluetooth and dual antenna and the (MIMO, Wi-Fi
8. **Alexa (the Word Phrase of Amazon Echo)** = Availability is Yes (Always-on / voice-activated / always-listening)
9. **Audio Quality of Amazon Echo** = 2 inch tweeter along with the 2.5 inch woofer and 360 - degree sound.

Chapter 03 -- Amazon Echo, Amazon Dot and Amazon Tap

The present world of the interlinked homes remains to be very detached mess. As Google and Apple compete with their own requirements — and other corporations are working the same with their own perspective — Amazon has very snuck within the attractive, part door with its intelligent, and sensible speaker. Other than that it also acts as a substitute, speakers. After greater than a year with just the Amazon Echo Dot to makes the way, the line of the Amazon intelligent audio system exemplifies that future. The tap, Echo, and Dot are very equivalent wise speakers, in that they participate in nearly the entire same capabilities, with minor variations.

If you're out there for a shrewd speaker however are not able to decide between these three leading speakers, here are the definite the key variations that will allow you to comprehend which speaker is satisfactory for you.

1. Amazon Echo:

The first and the foremost of its type, Amazon Echo is a 9 - inches speaker that at first look resembles a cylindrical shape or also as the Pringles tube. On the other hand, this unit is way over only a speaker that may able to play all the desiring and favorite tunes from Spotify, Pandora high song, and many others. (inform the speaker to Play the important Android Podcast, it will play it too) it may well conveniently come to be the smart supervisor to your house, linking to smart lights for instance the Philips Hue, Samsung Smart Things, Nest thermostats, and even more features.

Amazon's official Store service

It can be sincerely the smart phone research equipment without the display or any interface. It could be easily answer your questions, check site visitors, read books that are audio for you, and give updates about the weather, and well-nigh act as your sound-activated butler (except for sincerely bringing you a snack, and yet you can use it to order pizza or anything similar to that...).

In a slightly display or any type of creepy interface of semi-AI, the Echo is continually linked to Alexa of Amazon network, which is included in the cloud and consistently getting more and more smarter. The extra you utilize it, the extra it learns your speech patterns, preferences, and vocabulary, to raised give on what the user would requesting. It would be constantly learning.

2. Amazon Echo Dot:
1. **Availability of the Amazon Dot Echo** = Available in United States (Amazon United States order page) and also Available in the country of United Kingdom (Amazon United Kingdom order page)

2. **Release date in United States and United Kingdom** = in United States and in United Kingdom = September, 2016 .
3. **Dimensions** = 38 millimeter x 84 millimeter x 84 millimeter
4. **Price of Amazon Dot Echo** = in United States = $49, in United Kingdom = £49
5. **Weight of Amazon Dot Echo** = 250 in grams
6. **Power** = Plugs in any outlet of wall
7. **Connectivity of Amazon Dot Echo with other devices** = Dual-band, Bluetooth and dual antenna and the (MIMO, Wi-Fi
8. **Alexa (the Word Phrase of Amazon Dot Echo)** = Availability is Yes (Always-on / voice-activated / always-listening)
9. **Audio Quality of Amazon Dot Echo** = 2 inch tweeter along with the 2.5 inch woofer and 360 - degree sound.

The Dot is well-nigh the "Mini-Me of the Echo." It contains a smaller, quieter speaker and, in dimension, is extra comparable to a hockey percent. It can easily does the whole lot the Echo can do easily, but in addition contains a 3.5 millimeter output jack and also the little Bluetooth connectivity, permitting the user to attach it to their present sound process. Real, it could be easily as though anybody simply beheaded the Echo and then crumpled up the entire-measurement speaker and blocked it up into the neck, and growth, the Dot.

Hook up with and manipulate the whole sensible house instruments, as well as your current set-up of the audio system, creating the Dot perhaps probably the most fascinating of the family of the Amazon Echo, specifically for the reason that it can be most effective $50 (and proper, if the user happen to buy a 6-percent, he/she will have to only pay for five!).

3. **Amazon Tap:**
    1. **Release date of Amazon Tap** = 2016 in 31 March for United States
    2. **Availability of Amazon Tap** = Available in United States (Amazon United States order page)
    3. **Connectivity Provided:** supports 803.12 g, or 804.14 n and 812.15 b, Wi-Fi, Bluetooth
    4. **Power of Amazon Tap:** Depends on the Charging of its battery (approx. 9 to 10 hours of continually playback)
    5. **Dimensions of Amazon Tap** = 59 millimeter x 66 millimeter x 66 millimeter
    6. **Weight of the Amazon Tap** = 470 grams
    7. **Price of Amazon Tap** = in United States $129.99
    8. **Audio Quality** = 360 sound (dual 1.5 high inches drivers)
    9. **Alexa: the Work Phrase** = Availability is Present

The tap is the following inline tool and carries most of the similar points that the Echo contains, with the delivered advantage of portability. Along with as much as nine to ten hours of playback, the faucet has the feature of rechargeable and is derived with a helpful wireless charged cradle.

Considering the fact that it has the rechargeable battery-powered, the Amazon tap is not invariably always for listening purposes, so — because the title would endorse — you need to tap it to activate the work phrase of Alexa, which best works over the internet or Wi-Fi. It can be type of a discomfort within the keister.

Just like the Amazon Dot and Amazon Echo, the Amazon Tap can manipulate your shrewd house devices, since you'll ought to stand up and Amazon Tap it to take action (at that factor, the user could as good pull out their smart phones). The Amazon Tap could actually additionally act as the users' futuristic assistant, adding items to their daily calendar and serving to with new and novel searches. It makes links to their mobile and other smart instruments, like the tabs, by way of Bluetooth, however only for playback.

The Amazon Tap is the only relatively modifiable Amazon Echo option, along with the Amazon tap Sling cover to be had in approx. six to seven colors.

Chapter: 04 -- Privacy Concerns and Limitations of Amazon Echo Dot

Amazon manufacturer had been establishing inside Echo of its Lab126 places of work in Cambridge and Massachusetts, Silicon Valley, due to the fact at the least 2010 in definite levels of reports. This gadget used to be the part of Amazon that makes an attempt to develop its gadget portfolio before the e-reader known as Kindle. The Echo was featured in the first-ever tremendous Bowl Amazon e-reader advert in 2016. Hook up with and manipulate the whole sensible house instruments, as well as your current set-up of the audio system, creating the Dot perhaps probably the most fascinating of the family of the Amazon Echo, specifically for the reason that it can be most effective $50 (and proper, if the user happen to buy a 6-percent, he/she will have to only pay for five!).

Limitations:
Alexa boundaries can be learned in distinctive classes

1. **Quality of Sound** - straight evaluating the echo's sound exceptional compared with many other excessive qualities audio system falls brief, that being acknowledged the frictionless usage of voice that creates an expanded experience.

2. **Troublesome responsibilities** – the work phrase of Alexa at this time aren't capable to technique difficult commands comparable to `Alexa play and order the user the new Uber` it certainly omits and lacks the potential to manage a couple of instructions or difficult context based advantage

3. **Price** - there is a high-priced expense element of selling a $100 and -$ 180 units.

4. There are issues in regards to the entry Echo have to confidential conversations within the houses, or special signs of non-verbal tools that may determine what is present within the dwelling and who shouldn't be — established on perceptible cues similar to pace - tempo or television or radio programming.

5. The Amazon retorts to those problems via bringing up that the Amazon Echo most effective streams recordings from the consumer's residence while the 'wake phrase' prompts the Amazon Echo, although the machine is technically in a position of streaming sound recordings normally, and safely will regularly be taking note of realize if a customer has spoken any type of phrase or a single word.

6. Echo uses prior sound recordings the client has dispatched to the cloud carrier to beef up response to future questions the character would pose.

7. To handle privateer's considerations, the customer can erase the several sound recordings which could be also be presently related to the customers' account, nonetheless it may just reduce the person's potential utilizing voice search.

8. To erase these saved recordings, the consumer can search recommendation from manipulating of gadget web page on Amazon.Com or contact Amazon purchaser service.

Privacy Issues:

1. Echo makes use of the tackle set in the Alexa application when it wishes a region. Amazon and half of the party applications and websites use vicinity advantage to furnish position - established choices and retailer this knowledge to furnish voice offerings, the Maps app, to find the customers' device, and to notice the performance and correctness of region offerings.

2. Echo voice offerings use the consumer's situation to answer to the consumer's requests for neighborhood or outlets.

3. In a similar fashion, Echo makes use of the customer's vicinity to process the consumer's mapping-associated requests and fortify the experiences of maps.

4. All figuring out gathered is field to the Amazon.Com privateers become aware of Amazon retains digital recordings of buyers audio spoken after the "rise up phrase," and whereas the audio recordings are discipline to needs by way of legislation enforcement, govt. agents, and one of a kind entities by means of subpoena.

5. Amazon publishes some understanding in regards to the warrants it receives, the subpoenas that it may usually receive, and one of the warrants so much less demands it receives, enabling patrons some indication as to the percent of unlawful demands for client talents that it receives.

6. The present place of the device is ready to Seattle with the support of default and have acquired to be modified manually, however can most potent be set to a field inside the United States, Germany or United Kingdom. That is individual from smartphone-founded voice assistants that will get the precise position through by default GPS locators. This preclude can lead to apparently "mistaken" results for questions that propose the field just like "what is the climate" (around proper right here) or "make the alarm for 08:00 pm" (regional time correct right here).

7. This may occasionally enable Echo to report the proper time. There are two undesirable effects with making use of this approach. One is the flawed pm/am notation and the second is the mistaken date. Another more subtle work around is with the support of manipulating the data that can be easily transmitted and

obtained by means of Amazon's servers as described with the help of consumer "stone water" on the unofficial Amazon Echo discussion board. This approach produces right and exciting outcome. There are a couple of makes an try to bypass the United States most potent limit, exceptionally by using consumers in Australia and United States.

8. One such work around is to set the Echo to a time zone that is exactly 12 to 10 hours change from the neighborhood time. For illustration, if the present time in London is 10:40 am, the consumer can set Echo to Hawaii usual Time, which might be 10:40 pm. Nonetheless, it needs new technology with the support of Request Maker for Chrome to accomplish the mission. Interaction and conversation with Amazon Echo is presently best on hand in German and English.

Chapter: 05 -- Amazon Echo Dot vs. Echo

Amazon Echo Dot is approx. 360 speakers that has the ability of the ways discipline voice cognizance powered by the use of the Amazon Alexa voice provider as well as the assistant. For designing perspective, it appears like a hockey percentage with two buttons on top. It can be in specific fact a Bluetooth speaker that is similar to the first inch and a half of the perfect of a Pringles can.

The brand new Amazon Echo Dot contains everything the ancient Echo had, at the side of lengthy variety, some distance field voice capabilities, an motion button (for WiFi), a microphone off button, and of direction "Alexa," which can be reply questions, play tune, and offer you information, site visitors, climate, physical games outcome, and even much more. You would not be able for going to lose entry to any of the Echo's competencies, together with its 3rd party talents like Uber, Fitbit, Domino's Pizza, and Capitol One (decided within the Alexa application).

Nevertheless, there are a couple of gigantic variants among the historic Amazon Echo and the brand new Echo Dot, and these variations take the Dot previous its guardian product.

Key Differences of Amazon Echo Old and Amazon Dot new

S.no	Features	Amazon Echo Old	Amazon Dot new
1	"Alexa," which can easily play tune, reply questions, and provide the users with	Availability : Yes	Availability : Yes

	information, climate, visitors, physical activities outcome, and so on?		
2	Skills like Uber, Fitbit, and Domino's Pizza, (by way of Alexa)?	Availability : Yes	Availability : Yes
3	Lengthy variety, a ways - area voice capabilities?	Availability : Yes	Availability : Even Better
4	Availability of Action Button	Availability : Yes	Availability : Yes
5	Availability of Microphone Button	Availability : Yes	Availability : Yes
6	Availability of Speaker (Built-in)	Availability : Yes	Availability : Yes
7	Availability of Colors selections	Availability : Yes	Availability : Yes
8	Price	180 dollars	50 dollars
9	Feature of portability	Availability : No	Availability : Yes
10	A 3.5 millimeter audio output jack that enables linkage to any speaker and turns it into the work phrase of Alexa-enabled gadget?	Availability : No	Availability : Yes
11	Energy adapter and USB charging cable integrated?	Availability : Yes	Availability : Yes
12	Are you able to connect with your possess Bluetooth speaker?	Availability : No	Availability : Yes
13	ESP attribute designed for a few contraptions: phrase command indicators the closest machine?	Availability : No	Availability : Yes
14	Can you are taking it external with Amazon tap?	Availability : No	Availability : Yes
15	Activation of the hands-free with	Availability : Yes	Availability : Yes

	a wake phrase?		

At the same time the program of Echo Dot is much the same as its predecessor's, the hardware is much changed. That's what makes it exciting. This product comprises of a 3.5 millimeter audio system output jack that allows connectivity to any speaker and turns it into an Alexa enabled tools.

You could receive the good quality of sound that you may need and have an access of the work phrase of Alexa's smarts, comprising of the ESP function designed for a couple of contraptions. While you may say "Alexa", only the closest tools that the users are going to reply.

The Amazon Echo Dot is far smaller and lighter than the Amazon Echo, which raises its portability within the home. There are even many methods that would take the product of the external house if set with an extra work phrase of Alexa powered gadget called the Amazon tap.

Conclusion:

This eBook is a complete guide of Amazon Echo Dot which is also called as mission D or Doppler and shortened and known as Echo is a speaker and is designed through Amazon. Amazon Echo includes a 23.5 cm which is approx. 9.25 - inches speaker which has a shape like cylinder with a seven piece microphone display. The device retorts to the title "Alexa". This "wake phrase" will also be modified through the consumer to both "Amazon" and "Echo". This eBook contains the five sections, each sections has the guidelines of using the Amazon Echo dot and also key differences between the Amazon Dot, Amazon Echo and the Amazon Tap. The tap, Echo, and Dot are very equivalent wise speakers, in that they participate in nearly the entire same capabilities, with minor variations. The Amazon Echo Dot, similar to the Amazon Echo, presents hands-free activation by means of a wake phrase of Alexa. In that work phrase the app related to it and the spoken wake phrase that prompts the gadget can either be "Alexa", "Amazon" or "Echo,"

FREE Bonus Reminder

If you have not grabbed it yet, please go ahead and download your special bonus report *"DIY Projects. 13 Useful & Easy To Make DIY Projects To Save Money & Improve Your Home!"*

Simply Click the Button Below

OR **Go to This Page**

http://diyhomecraft.com/free

BONUS #2: More Free & Discounted Books or Products

Do you want to receive more Free/Discounted Books or Products?

We have a mailing list where we send out our new Books or Products when they go free or with a discount on Amazon. Click on the link below to sign up for Free & Discount Book & Product Promotions.

=> **Sign Up for Free & Discount Book & Product Promotions** <=

OR Go to this URL

http://zbit.ly/1WBb1Ek

CPSIA information can be obtained
at www.ICGtesting.com
Printed in the USA
LVOW10s1443050417
529721LV00009B/745/P